AVENGER

THOR

AVENGER

Collection Editor: *Cory Levine*
Editorial Assistants: *James Emmett & Joe Hochstein*
Assistant Editors: *Matt Masdeu, Alex Starbuck
& Nelson Ribeiro*
Editors, Special Projects: *Jennifer Grünwald
& Mark D. Beazley*
Senior Editor, Special Projects: *Jeff Youngquist*
Senior Vice President of Sales: *David Gabriel*
SVP of Brand Planning & Communications: *Michael Pasciullo*

Editor in Chief: *Axel Alonso*
Chief Creative Officer: *Joe Quesada*
Publisher: *Dan Buckley*
Executive Producer: *Alan Fine*

YOU ASK *HEIMDALL*, GUARDIAN OF THE RAINBOW BRIDGE OF ASGARD, WHAT HE KNOWS OF THE SONS OF ODIN, MIGHTY *THOR* AND CLEVER *LOKI?*

I, WHOSE EARS HEAR GRASS GROW AND WHOSE EYES CAN TRACK A SPARROW'S FLIGHT ACROSS THE HORIZON?

I KNOW *ALL.*

AND I CAN TELL YOU THAT THEY DID NOT ALWAYS TRUST EACH OTHER AS MUCH AS THEY DO NOW.

NO, THEIR FRIENDSHIP WAS TESTED--AND NEARLY *SHATTERED*--IN THEIR YOUTH, WHEN TIME ITSELF WAS YOUNG.

WHEN THEY FOUND THEMSELVES DUTY-BOUND TO CONQUER THE...

CITADEL OF SPIRES

"HERE WAS IMPRISONED THEIR DEAR COMRADE, *FANDRAL THE DASHING*, UPON HIS CAPTURE WHILE SPYING ON THE DARK ELVES' INFERNAL WAR MACHINES."

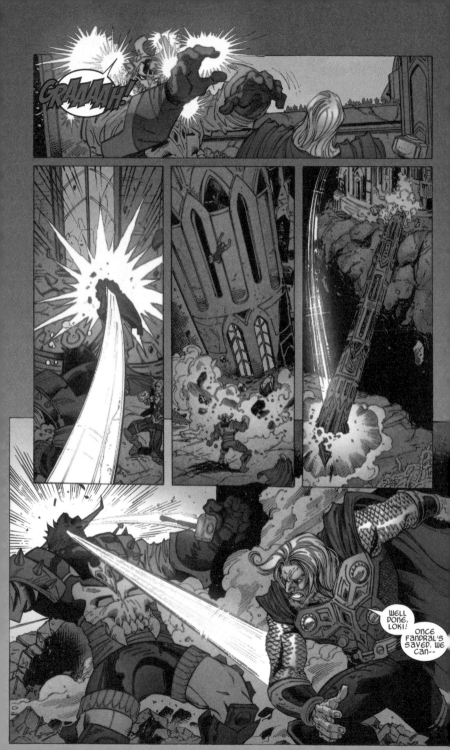

The End

I CAN USE THE SUB'S *COURSE CHARTS* TO RETRACE *LEVIATHAN'S* STEPS BACK TO HER HOME BASE, CAP, JUST AS WE PLANNED.

GOOD WORK, MORITA.

ALLIED INTELLIGENCE SAYS HYDRA IS BUILDING SOMETHING *BIG* AT THIS SECRET "U-BASE."

OUR JOB IS TO SHUT THEM *DOWN* BEFORE THIS NEW WEAPON--*WHATEVER* IT IS--IS DEPLOYED AGAINST OUR SOLDIERS IN THE FIELD.

YOU'RE OUR TACTICAL EXPERT, FALSWORTH--HOW DO YOU RECOMMEND WE PROCEED?

SURPRISE IS BLOODY WELL *CRUCIAL* TO THE SUCCESS OF MY PLAN, CAPTAIN.

SERGEANT *DUGAN,* YOU DIRECT SUPPRESSING FIRE FROM THE TOP OF THE SUBMARINE...

...WHILE *PERNIER* PLANTS THE EXPLOSIVES WE'LL USE TO MAKE THE UNDERGROUND GROTTO GO KABLOOEY...

...WITH ONE WELL-PLACED SHOT YOU IGNITE THE CHARGES, *JONES...*

...AND *MORITA* PLOTS OUR RETURN COURSE TO THE BRITISH BASE ON *GIBRALTAR.*

SOUNDS *EASY* JUST *TALKIN* ABOUT IT...

TRANQUILLITE... TOO QUIET!

HOW CAN WE BE SURE THE BASE'S GARRISON ISN'T JUST IN HIDING?

WE *CAN'T.* NOT UNTIL WE *SEARCH* THE PLACE.

DERNIER AND JONES, YOU TAKE THAT CORRIDOR DOWN THERE TO THE LEFT.

FALSWORTH AND MORITA, YOU TAKE THE RIGHT.

CAP, YOU AND I'LL...

CAP?

TYPICAL.

AND IT MUST HAVE HAD THE REST OF THE STAFF OF THIS DUMP FOR A *SNACK* BECAUSE THERE AIN'T NOBODY HERE BUT *US* AND IT.

I WAS ABLE TO WALTZ RIGHT IN AND OUT OF THE ENGINEERING DEPARTMENT WITH THE *PLANS* FOR THE WHOLE COMPLEX AND DIDN'T MEET ANYBODY BUT MY *SHADOW.*

OKAY. THE SUB-BASEMENT MUST BE THE FLOODED SECTION...ACTUALLY LOOKS RATHER SMALL...

OUI...

...IN FACT, MON CAPITAINE, I SHOULD BE ABLE TO PLANT SUFFICIENT CHARGES ON THE FLOOR OF THIS LEVEL TO DROP THE *CEILING* OF THIS BEAST'S LAIR DOWN ON *TOP* OF IT!

SOUNDS LIKE A PLAN, DERNIER.

BUT WE'RE GONNA HAVE TO FIRST GET MORITA AND FARNSWORTH OUT OF THERE--*IF* THEY'RE STILL *BREATHIN'.*

YOU UP FOR THAT, CAP'N?

ALWAYS.

OUR WATCHES ARE SYNCHRONIZED-- YOU GOT *THIRTY* MINUTES BEFORE WE BRING THE ROOF DOWN ON TENTACLE MONSTER.

LITERALLY.

UNDERSTOOD.

29 MIN

25 MIN

BLEEP

22 MIN

17 MIN

HELLLLOOOO?

GLOOPY RED SLIME MONSTER?

KARL

WILHELM

COME OUT, COME OUT WHEREVER YOU...

HMMM...

SEEMS LIKE A WEIRD PLACE FOR GRAFFITI...

HELFEN SIE MIR

JOSEPH

HANS

CAP? YOU COPY ME?

LOUD AND CLEAR, JONSEY.

I'VE TRANSLATED THE LAST FEW PAGES OF THE LEAD SCIENTIST'S JOURNAL, WHICH IS DATED JUST TWO DAYS AGO.

GO AHEAD.

APPARENTLY AN UNDERWATER EARTHQUAKE DAMAGED U-BASE, FLOODED THE SECTION YOU'RE IN NOW...

...AND CRACKED THE SEALS CONTAINING THE "HYDRA SERUM."

THE DOCTORS WERE CONCERNED SOME OF IT GOT INTO THE BASE'S WATER SUPPLY.

IS THAT HELPFUL TO YOU AT ALL?

The End

LONG, LONG AGO...

SUPPER! I DEMAND MY *SUPPER!!*

OR I SHALL TURN YOU ALL INTO *FROGS*-- EACH AND EVERY ONE OF YOU!

CAUSING A *RUCKUS,* MERLIN? *TSK, TSK.*

PAH! COME FOR ANOTHER *GLOAT,* HAVE YOU?

NOT *STILL* UPSET ABOUT THE BELT? COME COME, I'VE BEEN CHANNELLING YOUR MAGIC WITH IT FOR *WEEKS* NOW. CAN'T WE LET BYGONES BE BYGONES?

YOU CAN'T *BEGIN* TO CONTROL THAT BELT! IT CONTAINS MORE *POWER* THAN YOU CAN *POSSIBLY* IMAGINE!

OH, DON'T THINK POORLY OF ME. WHY, WE'RE TWO SIDES OF THE *SAME COIN,* YOU AND I.

OF COURSE, WHEN *HEADS* IS SHOWING, *TAILS* HAS TO LIE FACE DOWN IN THE *DIRT.* THAT'S THE THING ABOUT COINS. *SO* UNFAIR.

ANYTHING INTERESTING, EARL?

COULD BE... THIS DOOR IS SEALED. I'M ASSUMING THERE'S SOMETHING IMPORTANT BEHIND IT.

LET'S GET YANKEE DOODLE DOO IN HERE.

'EY! FIGHTING AMERICAN! THIS WAY!

"FIGHTING AMERICAN"?

THIS DOOR...IT BODES.

BODES? BODES WHAT?

NOTHIN' IN PARTICULAR. JUST GENERALLY... BODES.

WANNA USE YOUR GIZMO ON IT?

WORTH A SHOT.

TODAY, BERGEN, OKLAHOMA. THE BERGEN WAR MEMORIAL MUSEUM.

OKAY... ANY IDEAS WHAT *THIS* ONE IS?

THAT IS A *BELT BUCKLE...* NO, WAIT. A *CENTERPIECE* FOR A *SHIELD.*

YOU SURE?

NO. NOT REALLY.

SORRY, THOR. I THOUGHT YOU'D BE *GOOD* AT THIS. THESE ARE MAINLY *NORDIC* ARTIFACTS, RIGHT?

THEY ARE *EARTH* ARTIFACTS. AND I AM NOT OF EARTH.

YEAH.

YOU SEEM *SHORT OF TEMPER* TONIGHT, JANE. IS SOMETHING WRONG?

I...I GOT A LETTER FROM MY BROTHER HAL, ASKING FOR *MONEY.* HE'S IN A *FIX...* BUT IT'S HIS *OWN FAULT,* GAMBLING, AND IT'S NOT LIKE I HAVE IT TO SPARE.

IT'S NOT THE *FIRST* TIME, EITHER. UNTIL NOW I'VE ALWAYS SAID *NO...*

...BUT NOW I'M WONDERING IF THAT WAS THE RIGHT THING TO DO.

WHAT DO *YOU* THINK, THOR?

THOR?

YOU *YELLED.*

AS DID YOU.

IT...SEEMS WE SHARE A PREDICAMENT. I AM *THOR,* SON OF ODIN.

CAPTAIN AMERICA. YOU... *THOR? REALLY?*

REALLY. SO I AM STILL IN *AMERICA...*

SO I'M IN *SCANDINAVIA...*

I JUST GOT HERE... *UNEXPECTEDLY.* WHAT'S YOUR EXCUSE?

HOLD ON, *DUCK!*

FLUMP

I THOUGHT I SAW A *GLINT OF LIGHT* THAT SHOULDN'T BE THERE. I WAS *RIGHT.*

AN... *ASSASSIN?*

LOOKS LIKE IT.

CLOP CLOP CLO PCLOP CLOP CLOP CL

AND THAT... IS PROBABLY HIS *QUARRY.*

THERE MAY BE *MORE* OF THESE GUYS--RUN AHEAD AND *STOP THOSE HORSES* WHILE I...

HOLD.

THHDOOMM!

WHUMP

WHUMP

WHUMP

WHUMP

WHUMP

I TRUST THAT WILL BE *SUFFICIENT*, CAPTAIN...

CAPTAIN?

JUST A MOMENT, THOR...

CAMELOT 10 Miles

...I THINK I MIGHT KNOW WHERE WE *ARE*.

AND **YOU**, MERLIN... YOU SEEM NOW TO HAVE COMPLETELY **RECOVERED** FROM YOUR...WHAT DID YOU CALL IT...?

MY **REGENERATION**, SIRE?

THAT'S IT! I ADMIT, THE **NEW FACE** TOOK A LITTLE GETTING USED TO...BUT I AM PLEASED TO SEE YOUR **POWER** AND **LEARNING** REMAIN UNDIMINISHED!

YOUR MAJESTY IS TOO KIND.

WHAT **NONSENSE** IS THIS, LOKI? HE THINKS YOU ARE **SOMEONE ELSE**!

DON'T **BLOW** THIS FOR ME, BRO. THIS IS A **GREAT GIG**. WHAT ARE YOU **DOING** HERE, ANYWAY?

SOME SORT OF...**MAGICAL ACCIDENT**, I BELIEVE. AND **YOU**?

SNAP! I CRACKED OPEN AN ANCIENT BOOK I PROBABLY **SHOULDN'T** HAVE... AND **WOUND UP** HERE. THAT WAS A **FEW MONTHS** AGO.

FOUND MY FEET PRETTY FAST, THOUGH. ALWAYS DO.

SEE THIS **BELT**? **MAGIC**. AND YOU THOUGHT YOUR **CELLPHONE** WAS HOT STUFF...

YOU SHOULD BE MORE **CAREFUL**, MY BROTHER. YOUR CONSTANT **MEDDLING** WITH MYSTIC **FORCES**...

...MAY ONE DAY BE THE **DEATH** OF YOU.

LISTEN, **GOLDILOCKS**. I'VE GOT PLANS HERE--A **FUTURE**, EVEN--AND IF YOU GET IN MY **WAY**... I **WILL** STOP YOU.

I **SINCERELY** HOPE YOU DO NOT **THREATEN** ME, LOKI. I WOULD HATE TO--

RUUUMMMMMBBLLLL

HOLD! WHAT SORCERY IS THIS?

RRAAARRRRRRRR

A...A **DRAGON!** IN THE NAME OF OUR LORD...IS SUCH A THING **POSSIBLE?**

SIRE...I SUGGEST WE SAVE THE **PHILOSOPHY**--

TAWOCK

SCHWARRR

--FOR AFTER THE **FUNERAL!**

TER-RIFIC.

DON'T DO THAT AG--

TWARK

HOLD! *HOLD*, MY BEAUTIES!

THEY'RE *BATTERED*-- BUT *ALIVE*.

IT'S *DOWN* TO *YOU, ME* AND *MERLIN*.

MERLIN?

HIS NAME IS *LOKI*, NOT MERLIN-- AND HE HAS *DESERTED* US! I--

OF COURSE! THE DRAGON... THE ASSASSINS... HE *KNEW*! HE *KNEW*!

AND HE HAS *TAKEN THE GRAIL*!

WE MAY NEED HIS POWER TO *STOP* THIS THING. HE CAN'T HAVE GONE FAR...CAN YOU *HOLD IT OFF* FOR A WHILE?

CAPTAIN! I AM *THOR, SON OF ODIN*!

YES OR NO?

THWAAMM

SILLY QUESTION.

OD'S BLOOD! WHAT TRICKERY IS THIS...?

GONE! A MERE *SHADOW*... A *CONSTRUCT* OF LOKI'S *MAGIC*!

AT LAST-- IT'S *MINE!* THE *ULTIMATE SOURCE OF POWER!*

IT'S THE DREAM OF EVERY MAGICIAN SINCE *THE DAWN OF TIME--* THE ABILITY TO HAVE EVERY COMMAND... *EVERY SLIGHTEST WISH...*INSTANTLY, INFALLIBLY *OBEYED!*

AND NOW IT LOOKS LIKE RAIN.

THIS DAY JUST GETS BETTER AND BETTER.

CAPTAIN! IVE BEEN!

THOR! WHAT...?

CAN'T *HEAR* YOU...!

AAGH!

SMART... YET STRANGELY *STUPID!* YOU THINK I STILL NEED MERLIN'S POWER NOW I HAVE THE *GRAIL?* I--

AAAHHH!

LOKI--YOU ARE A *FOOL!* DID YOU THINK THE BELT WAS THE *SOURCE* OF MY POWER?

IT WAS *NEVER* THE SOURCE! IT WAS THE *DAMPER*...THE *CONTAINER!* AS LONG AS IT EXISTED SOMEWHERE IN THIS WORLD, MY ABILITIES WERE LIMITED TO MERE *PARLOR TRICKS!* WITHOUT IT...

...*I AM GREAT AND TERRIBLE!*

I...CANNOT STAY LIKE THIS FOR LONG. WHEN MY POWER IS *UNHARNESSED*, IT CAN *DEVOUR* ME. I MUST FIND SOME NEW VESSEL OF CONTAINMENT *URGENTLY*.

BUT *FIRST*...

BEHOLD! THE KING AND HIS LOYAL KNIGHT... *RESTORED TO HEALTH!*

M-MERLIN...?

AND NOW...MY *RESCUERS*. THE CUP WAS TO BRING ME A *CHAMPION*--HONEST, *BRAVE* AND TRUE. IT APPEARS MY ENCHANTMENT WAS EVEN *MORE* EFFECTIVE THAN I HAD HOPED.

BUT YOU DO NOT *BELONG* HERE... AND THUS IT IS TIME FOR ME TO SEND YOU *HOME.*

HOME... WITH MY *ETERNAL* GRATITUDE.

IT WOULD BE MY HONOR TO MEET YOU *AGAIN* ONE DAY, CAPTAIN.

THOR-- THE HONOR WAS ALL...

SUCH CHAMPIONS, *INDEED.*

THEY MAY BE *GONE*...BUT THEY SHALL NOT BE *FORGOTTEN.* I SHALL SEE TO THAT.

THOR?

THOR, ARE YOU EVEN *LISTENING* TO ME?

I, AHH...OF *COURSE*, JANE, I...

LIAR. BUT YOU'RE *CUTE*, SO YOU GET AWAY WITH IT.

OH, HEY, I JUST REMEMBERED SOMETHING...

...CHECK *THIS* OUT.

I'D SWEAR THAT THIS WAS *YOU* IN YOUR *COLORFUL PAST*... EXCEPT, GIVEN THE OTHER GUY'S WEARING AN *AMERICAN FLAG* A THOUSAND YEARS TOO EARLY, IT *HAS* TO BE A FAKE.

STILL... PRETTY COOL, RIGHT?

ANYWAY... WHAT DO YOU THINK? SHOULD I *HELP* HAL OR *NOT*?

HELP HIM? I...

YES, YES, JANE...

...HELP YOUR BROTHER.

THAT WOULD MAKE ME *VERY HAPPY* INDEED.

THE END

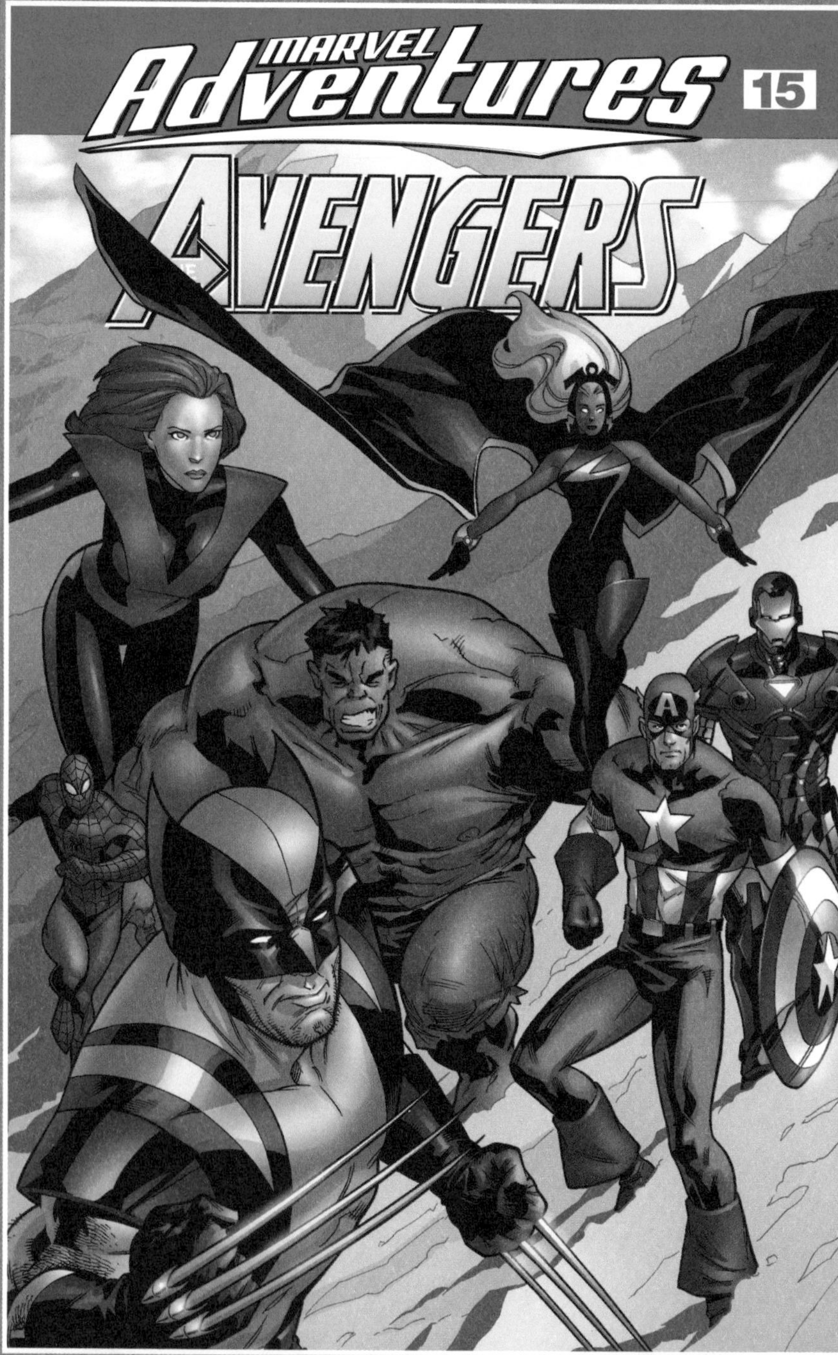
MARVEL
Adventures
15
AVENGERS